THE INDIAN MIDDLE-CLASS AND THEIR INVESTMENT DILLEMA

Navigating Financial Choices Amidst Aspirations and Realities

Bhavesh Parmar

CONTENTS

Title Page
Chapter 1: The Evolution of the Indian Middle Class | 1
Chapter 2: Understanding the Investment Dilemma | 7
Chapter 3: Spectrum of Investment Options | 12
Chapter 4: Influence of Education and Financial Literacy | 17
Chapter 5: The Impact of Government Policies on Investment Decisions | 22
Chapter 6: Real Estate: A Favoured but Risky Bet | 27
Chapter 7: The Rise of Mutual Funds and Stock Markets in India | 32
Chapter 8: Gold: The Traditional Safe Haven | 37
Chapter 9: The Challenge of Retirement Planning | 42
Chapter 10: The Role of Technology and Digital Platforms | 48
Chapter 11: Women and Investment: A Growing Influence | 54
Chapter 12: The Future of Investment in India | 60
About The Author | 83

Introduction

The Indian middle class, often described as the backbone of the nation's economy, has undergone a significant transformation over the past few decades. With rising incomes, better education, and increasing aspirations, this segment of the population has become a crucial driver of India's growth story. However, along with these advancements comes a complex dilemma: the question of where and how to invest their hard-earned money. This book explores the various dimensions of this dilemma, analysing the factors that influence investment decisions, the challenges faced by the Indian middle class, and the evolving landscape of investment opportunities.

Chapter 1: The Evolution of the Indian Middle Class

This chapter traces the historical growth of the Indian middle class, from its nascent stages in post-independence India to its current status as a significant economic force. It examines the social, economic, and political changes that have contributed to the rise of this demographic, highlighting the increasing disposable income and shifting aspirations that define the modern Indian middle class.

Chapter 2: Understanding the Investment Dilemma

In this chapter, we delve into the psychological and cultural factors that contribute to the investment dilemma faced by the Indian middle class. The fear of losing hard-earned money, the desire for financial security, and the pressure to maintain or improve social status all play a role in shaping investment decisions. This chapter also explores how traditional attitudes towards savings and investments have evolved over time.

Chapter 3: The Spectrum of Investment Options

This chapter provides a comprehensive overview of the various investment options available to the Indian middle class, ranging from traditional choices like fixed deposits and gold to more modern avenues such as mutual funds, stocks, real estate, and cryptocurrencies. Each investment type is discussed in detail, considering its risk profile, potential returns, and suitability for different financial goals.

Chapter 4: The Influence of Education and Financial Literacy

Education and financial literacy are critical factors in the investment decisions of the Indian middle class. This chapter explores how access to education and awareness of financial products impact investment choices. It also examines the role of financial advisors, the growing importance of digital platforms, and the influence of social media on investment behavior.

Chapter 5: The Impact of Government Policies

Government policies, regulations, and economic reforms have a profound impact on the investment landscape in India. This chapter analyses the role of tax incentives, subsidies, and regulatory frameworks in shaping investment decisions. It also considers the impact of economic policies, such as demonetization and the introduction of the Goods and Services Tax (GST), on the investment patterns of the middle class.

Chapter 6: Real Estate: A Favoured but Risky Bet

For many in the Indian middle class, real estate is the ultimate investment goal. This chapter examines the allure of property investment, the risks involved, and the challenges posed by fluctuating market conditions, regulatory hurdles, and the availability of affordable housing. It also explores the emotional and cultural significance of owning property in India.

Chapter 7: The Rise of Mutual Funds and Stock Markets

The Indian stock market and mutual funds have gained significant traction among the middle class in recent years. This chapter explores the factors driving this trend, including the influence of financial education campaigns, improved market access through digital platforms, and the search for higher returns in a low-interest-rate environment. It also discusses the risks associated with equity investments and the importance of a diversified portfolio.

Chapter 8: Gold: The Traditional Safe Haven

Gold has been a preferred investment for generations in India, symbolizing wealth and security. This chapter delves into the cultural and historical reasons behind the Indian middle class's continued fascination with gold, despite the emergence of other investment options. It also discusses the pros and cons of investing in gold in the modern context.

Chapter 9: The Challenge of Retirement Planning

Retirement planning poses a significant challenge for the Indian middle class, given the lack of a comprehensive social security system. This chapter explores the importance of long-term financial planning, the role of pension schemes, and the challenges faced by individuals in balancing current expenses with future needs.

Chapter 10: The Role of Technology and Digital Platforms

The advent of technology has revolutionized the investment landscape in India. This chapter examines the role of digital platforms, mobile apps, and robo-advisors in making investment more accessible to the middle class. It also discusses the benefits and risks associated with these technological advancements, including the potential for fraud and the need for cybersecurity.

Chapter 11: Women and Investment: A Growing Influence

The role of women in investment decisions is evolving, with more women becoming financially independent and taking an active interest in managing their finances. This chapter explores the unique challenges and opportunities faced by women in the Indian middle class, including the influence of gender norms, the growing importance of financial education for women, and the rise of women-specific investment products.

Chapter 12: The Future of Investment in India

This concluding chapter looks at the future of investment for the Indian middle class, considering emerging trends such as sustainable investing, the impact of climate change on investment decisions, and the potential for new financial products and services. It also discusses the importance of continued financial education and the need for government policies that support the financial well-being of the middle class.

Conclusion

The Indian middle class stands at a crossroads, facing both unprecedented opportunities and significant challenges in their quest for financial security and growth. This book has sought to explore the complex and evolving landscape of investment for this crucial demographic, offering insights into the factors that influence their decisions and the strategies they can employ to navigate their financial futures. As India continues to grow and change, so too will the investment dilemmas faced by the middle class, making it ever more important to stay informed, adaptable, and resilient in the face of uncertainty.

CHAPTER 1: THE EVOLUTION OF THE INDIAN MIDDLE CLASS

Introduction

The Indian middle class has undergone a profound transformation from its modest beginnings in the post-independence era to its current status as a major economic force. This chapter traces the historical development of the Indian middle class, examining the social, economic, and political changes that have shaped its growth. By exploring the factors that have contributed to the rise of this demographic, we gain insights into the increasing disposable income and shifting aspirations that define the modern Indian middle class.

Historical Overview

1. **Early Post-Independence Era (1947-1980)**

   a. **Emergence of the Middle Class**

   In the early years following India's independence in 1947, the middle class was relatively small and predominantly comprised bureaucrats, professionals, and small business owners. The economy was characterized by state control and protectionism, with a focus on self-sufficiency and industrialization. The middle class during this period was primarily urban and limited in its economic reach, with consumption patterns largely dictated by necessity rather than affluence. Therefore, the middle class was characterized by a modest standard of living and limited access to consumer goods.

b. Economic Policies and Growth

During the Nehruvian era, economic policies were centered around socialist principles and self-sufficiency. The emphasis was on public sector-led growth and protectionist trade policies. These policies contributed to a controlled and slow-growing economy, which limited the expansion of the middle class. Nonetheless, this period laid the groundwork for future growth by establishing a foundation of public education and healthcare.

2. Economic Liberalization and Growth (1980-2000)

a. Liberalization Era

The economic liberalization of the 1990s marked a turning point for the Indian middle class. The 1991 economic reforms, initiated by then-Finance Minister Manmohan Singh, aimed to reduce state control, encourage private investment, and integrate India into the global economy. These reforms led to rapid economic growth, increased foreign investment, and the emergence of new industries.

b. Rise in Disposable Income

The liberalization era brought about a significant increase in disposable income for many Indians. The expansion of sectors such as information technology, telecommunications, and finance created numerous high-paying jobs and opportunities for upward mobility. This period also saw a surge in consumerism, with the middle-class gaining access to a broader range of goods and services, including luxury items and international brands.

c. Changing Aspirations

The economic boom of the 1990s and 2000s led to shifting aspirations within the middle class. There was a growing emphasis on education, career advancement, and improved living standards. Aspirations expanded beyond basic needs to include home ownership, higher education, and leisure activities. This period also saw a rise in entrepreneurial ventures and increased participation in the stock market and real estate investments.

3. Modern Era and Emerging Trends (2000-Present)

a. Expansion and Diversification

The 21st century has witnessed continued expansion and diversification of the Indian middle class. The growth of urban centers, increased access to education, and technological advancements have contributed to the rise of a more affluent and diversified middle class. According to a 2023 report by the McKinsey Global Institute, the Indian middle class is expected to comprise over 600 million people by 2030, making it one of the largest consumer markets in the world.

b. Digital Revolution

The digital revolution has played a crucial role in shaping the modern Indian middle class. The proliferation of smartphones, internet access, and digital financial services has transformed consumption patterns and investment behaviors. Online shopping, digital payments, and fintech solutions have become integral to daily life, further enhancing the middle class's economic participation and financial capabilities.

c. Emerging Aspirations

Contemporary aspirations of the Indian middle class reflect a focus on quality of life, personal fulfillment, and global connectivity. There is a growing emphasis on health and wellness, experiential consumption, and sustainable living. The middle class is increasingly seeking to balance professional success with personal well-being and social responsibility.

Social and Economic Impacts

1. Urbanization and Lifestyle Changes

The growth of the middle class has been closely linked to urbanization. As more people move to cities and metropolitan areas, there has been a shift towards a more urban-centric lifestyle. This includes changes in housing, transportation, and consumption patterns. The demand for modern amenities, better infrastructure, and improved public services has increased.

2. Education and Employment

The rise of the middle class has led to greater emphasis on education and skill development. Higher educational attainment and specialized training have become key factors in achieving upward mobility. The job market has diversified, with increased opportunities in sectors such as IT, finance, healthcare, and entrepreneurship.

3. Political and Social Influence

The expanding middle class has also increased its political and social influence. With greater economic power comes a stronger voice in political and social issues. The middle class is playing a more active role in advocacy for social change, environmental sustainability, and governance reforms.

Challenges and Future Outlook

1. Income Inequality

Despite the growth of the middle class, income inequality remains a significant challenge. The benefits of economic growth have not been evenly distributed, and there is a growing disparity between the upper middle class and the lower income segments. Addressing income inequality and ensuring inclusive growth will be critical for sustaining the progress of the middle class.

2. Economic Volatility

The Indian economy faces periodic volatility due to global economic conditions, policy changes, and domestic challenges. Economic stability and resilience will be important for maintaining the growth trajectory of the middle class and ensuring continued progress.

3. Sustainability and Social Responsibility

As the middle class grows and evolves, there is a growing focus on sustainability and social responsibility. The demand for environmentally friendly products, ethical business practices, and corporate social responsibility is expected to shape future investment and consumption patterns.

Conclusion

The evolution of the Indian middle class has been marked by significant social, economic, and political changes. From its modest beginnings in the post-independence era to its current status as a major economic force, the middle class has played a pivotal role in shaping India's growth and development. As the middle class continues to expand and diversify, it will face new challenges and opportunities. Understanding this evolution provides valuable insights into the dynamics of India's economic and social landscape, highlighting the ongoing transformation of one of the world's most dynamic and influential demographics.

CHAPTER 2: UNDERSTANDING THE INVESTMENT DILEMMA

Introduction

The Indian middle class faces a distinct investment dilemma characterized by a blend of psychological, cultural, and social factors. This chapter delves into the underlying reasons for this dilemma, including fears about losing hard-earned money, the quest for financial security, and the pressures associated with social status. Additionally, we explore how traditional attitudes towards savings and investments have evolved over time.

Psychological Factors

1. Fear of Losing Hard-Earned Money

a. Behavioral Economics and Loss Aversion

The fear of losing money is a significant psychological barrier for many investors. According to behavioural economics, "loss aversion" describes how the pain of losing money is more intense than the pleasure of gaining an equivalent amount. This aversion can lead individuals to avoid investments perceived as risky, preferring safer options despite potentially lower returns. For many in the Indian middle class, this fear is intensified by the value placed on financial stability and the historical context of economic uncertainties.

b. Impact of Historical Economic Instability

India's economic history, marked by periods of

instability and uncertainty, has influenced collective attitudes towards financial risk. Prior experiences of economic downturns and crises have left a lasting impact, fostering a cautious approach towards investments. This historical context reinforces the preference for safe, low-risk investment options over more volatile ones.

2. **Desire for Financial Security**

   a. **Importance of Stability**

   Financial security is a central concern for the Indian middle class. The absence of a comprehensive social security system means that individuals must rely on personal savings and investments to secure their future. This emphasis on security drives a preference for investment options that promise stable and predictable returns, such as fixed deposits and government-backed schemes.

   b. **Family Obligations and Expectations**

   Cultural expectations and family obligations also play a role in shaping investment decisions. The need to provide for extended family members and fulfil social responsibilities can pressure individuals to prioritize safe investments that ensure long-term stability over potentially higher but riskier returns.

3. **Pressure to Maintain or Improve Social Status**

   a. **Social Status and Investment Choices**

   In Indian society, social status is often linked to visible markers of success, such as property ownership and luxury goods. This pressure to display economic success can influence investment choices, leading individuals to invest in high-profile assets or ventures to enhance or maintain their social standing, even if they are not the most financially prudent.

b. Role of Social Networks

Social networks and peer influences further shape investment behavior. The desire to conform to social norms or gain validation from peers can lead individuals to make investment decisions based on trends or societal expectations rather than personal financial goals and risk tolerance.

Evolution of Traditional Attitudes

1. Traditional Savings Practices

a. Historical Preferences

Traditionally, savings in India have been oriented towards physical assets like gold and real estate. These practices reflect a cultural preference for tangible assets perceived as secure and valuable. Gold, in particular, has been viewed as a symbol of wealth and financial safety, deeply embedded in cultural and historical contexts.

b. Government Schemes

Government-backed savings schemes such as the Public Provident Fund (PPF) and National Savings Certificate (NSC) have historically been popular among the Indian middle class. These schemes offer guaranteed returns and are perceived as low-risk options, aligning with traditional attitudes towards financial security.

2. Emergence of Modern Investment Options

a. Impact of Economic Liberalization

The economic liberalization of the 1990s introduced a range of new investment options, including stocks, mutual funds, and bonds. This shift challenged traditional attitudes and provided opportunities for diversifying investments. However, the transition has been gradual, with many individuals maintaining traditional practices alongside newer options.

b. Growing Financial Literacy

Increased financial literacy and access to investment education have contributed to changing attitudes. Modern financial education programs and digital platforms have made it easier for individuals to explore and understand diverse investment options. This has led to a gradual shift towards more varied investment strategies, though traditional preferences still persist.

Addressing the Investment Dilemma

1. Enhancing Financial Literacy

a. Role of Education

Financial education plays a crucial role in addressing the investment dilemma. Educating individuals about risk management, diversification, and investment strategies can help mitigate fears and promote informed decision-making. Financial literacy programs should focus on practical aspects of investing, helping individuals balance risk and return.

b. Role of Financial Advisors

Financial advisors can provide valuable guidance by offering personalized advice and helping clients align their investments with their financial goals and risk tolerance. Advisors can assist in developing a diversified investment portfolio that addresses individual fears and aspirations.

2. Promoting Balanced Investment Strategies

a. Encouraging Diversification

Encouraging diversification is key to managing investment risks. A diversified portfolio can help mitigate the impact of market volatility and reduce the overall risk of loss. By spreading investments across different asset classes, individuals can achieve a balance between risk and return.

b. Shifting Attitudes

To address the investment dilemma, it is essential to shift attitudes towards risk and return. Emphasizing the importance of long-term financial planning and the potential benefits of different investment options can help individuals make more balanced and rational investment decisions.

Conclusion

The investment dilemma faced by the Indian middle class is influenced by a range of psychological, cultural, and social factors. The fear of losing money, the quest for financial security, and societal pressures all play a role in shaping investment decisions. Traditional attitudes towards savings and investments have evolved over time, reflecting changes in economic conditions and financial education. Understanding these factors is crucial for addressing the investment dilemma and promoting more informed and balanced investment strategies.

CHAPTER 3: SPECTRUM OF INVESTMENT OPTIONS

Introduction

The Indian middle class has a diverse array of investment options available, reflecting both traditional and modern financial tools. This chapter provides a comprehensive overview of these investment options, detailing their risk profiles, potential returns, and suitability for different financial goals. By understanding these various options, investors can make informed decisions that align with their financial objectives.

Traditional Investment Options

1. Fixed Deposits (FDs)

a. Overview

Fixed Deposits (FDs) are one of the most traditional and popular investment options in India. Investors deposit a lump sum amount with a bank or financial institution for a specified tenure, during which interest is earned at a fixed rate.

b. Risk Profile

FDs are considered low-risk investments. They offer guaranteed returns and the safety of principal, making them ideal for conservative investors. The risk is minimal as they are backed by the bank and insured up to a certain limit.

c. Potential Returns

Returns on FDs are generally modest compared to other investment options, typically ranging between 5% and 7% per annum, depending on the institution and tenure.

d. Suitability

FDs are ideal for short- to medium-term financial goals, such as building an emergency fund or saving for specific expenses. They provide predictable returns and ensure the safety of the principal amount.

2. Gold

a. Overview

Gold has long been a preferred investment in India for centuries, valued for its cultural significance and perceived stability. Investment in gold can be made through physical gold (jewellery, coins, bars) or financial instruments like Gold ETFs and Sovereign Gold Bonds.

b. Risk Profile

Gold is considered a relatively safe asset, though its price can be volatile. Factors influencing gold prices include global economic conditions, currency fluctuations, and geopolitical tensions.

c. Potential Returns

Historically, gold has served as a good hedge against inflation and currency devaluation. While it does not generate income like interest or dividends, it provides capital appreciation potential.

d. Suitability

Gold is suitable for long-term investors looking to preserve wealth and hedge against inflation. It is also a good option for diversifying an investment portfolio.

Modern Investment Options

1. Mutual Funds

a. Overview

Mutual funds pool capital from multiple investors to

invest in a diversified portfolio of assets, including stocks, bonds, or other securities. They are managed by professional fund managers who make investment decisions on behalf of investors.

b. Risk Profile

The risk associated with mutual funds varies depending on the type of fund. Equity funds are higher risk with the potential for higher returns, while debt funds are lower risk with more stable returns.

c. Potential Returns

Returns on mutual funds depend on the underlying assets and market conditions. Equity mutual funds can provide higher returns but come with greater volatility. Debt funds offer more stable, though generally lower returns.

d. Suitability

Mutual funds are suitable for investors seeking diversification and professional management. They cater to various financial goals, including retirement planning, wealth accumulation, and tax savings.

2. Stocks

a. Overview

Investing in stocks involves buying shares of individual companies, giving investors ownership and the potential to earn dividends.

b. Risk Profile

Stocks are high-risk investments due to their volatility. Prices can fluctuate based on company performance, market conditions, and economic factors.

c. Potential Returns

Stocks offer the potential for significant returns through capital appreciation and dividends. However, they come with the risk of substantial losses.

d. Suitability

Stocks are suitable for investors with a higher risk tolerance and a long-term investment horizon. They are appropriate for wealth creation and capital growth.

3. Real Estate

a. Overview

Real estate investments involve purchasing property with the aim of generating rental income or capital appreciation. This category includes residential, commercial, and industrial properties.

b. Risk Profile

Real estate investments carry risks related to market fluctuations, property maintenance, and liquidity. The real estate market can be cyclical, with periods of high and low growth.

c. Potential Returns

Real estate can provide stable rental income and potential capital gains. Returns vary based on location, property type, and market conditions.

d. Suitability

Real estate is suitable for investors looking for long-term investments and those seeking tangible assets. It is also a good option for generating passive income.

4. Cryptocurrencies

a. Overview

Cryptocurrencies are digital assets that use blockchain technology for secure transactions. Popular cryptocurrencies include Bitcoin, Ethereum, and various altcoins.

b. Risk Profile

Cryptocurrencies are highly volatile and speculative investments. Their value can fluctuate dramatically due to market sentiment, regulatory developments, and technological advancements.

c. Potential Returns

Cryptocurrencies have shown potential for high returns, but they come with significant risk. Returns can be unpredictable, and the market is relatively new and evolving.

d. Suitability

Cryptocurrencies are suitable for investors with a high-risk tolerance and an interest in emerging technologies. They are not recommended for conservative investors or those with short-term financial goals.

Conclusion

The spectrum of investment options available to the Indian middle class encompasses a range of traditional and modern avenues, each with distinct characteristics. From the stability of fixed deposits and gold to the dynamic potential of mutual funds, stocks, real estate, and cryptocurrencies, understanding these options allows investors to tailor their strategies to their financial goals and risk tolerance. A well-informed approach to investing can help achieve long-term financial success and stability.

CHAPTER 4: INFLUENCE OF EDUCATION AND FINANCIAL LITERACY

Introduction

Education and financial literacy are pivotal in shaping the investment decisions of the Indian middle class. The ability to understand financial products, assess risks, and make informed choices greatly influences investment behavior. This chapter explores the impact of education and financial literacy on investment decisions, the role of financial advisors, the growing significance of digital platforms, and the influence of social media on investment behavior.

The Role of Education and Financial Literacy

1. Impact on Investment Decisions

a. Understanding Financial Products

Education equips individuals with the knowledge required to understand various financial products, from fixed deposits to complex derivatives. A higher level of financial literacy enables investors to evaluate investment options critically, understand the associated risks, and make informed decisions.

b. Risk Assessment and Management

Financial literacy helps investors assess and manage risks effectively. Educated investors are more likely to diversify their portfolios, select suitable investment instruments, and avoid high-risk schemes that could jeopardize their financial well-being.

c. Long-Term Financial Planning

Knowledge of financial planning principles allows individuals to set realistic financial goals and develop strategies to achieve them. This includes understanding the importance of saving, investing for retirement, and managing debt.

2. Access to Financial Education

a. Formal Education

Financial education is increasingly being integrated into formal education systems, including schools and universities. This integration helps students understand basic financial concepts, such as budgeting, saving, and investing, early in their lives.

b. Financial Literacy Programs

Various organizations and government initiatives offer financial literacy programs aimed at enhancing the financial knowledge of the general public. These programs often focus on practical financial skills and investment strategies.

c. Online Resources

The availability of online resources such as financial blogs, e-learning platforms, and webinars has significantly enhanced access to financial education. These resources provide valuable information on various investment options and financial strategies.

The Role of Financial Advisors

Guidance and Expertise

Financial advisors play a crucial role in helping individuals navigate complex financial markets. They provide personalized investment advice, helping clients build diversified portfolios and optimize their investment strategies.

a. Tailored Investment Strategies

Advisors assess clients' financial goals, risk tolerance, and investment preferences to recommend suitable investment options. Their expertise can help investors make informed decisions and avoid common pitfalls (FPA, 2023).

b. Ongoing Support and Education

Financial advisors also offer ongoing support and education, helping clients stay informed about market changes and adjust their strategies accordingly. This ongoing relationship ensures that investment decisions remain aligned with clients' evolving financial goals.

Influence of Digital Platforms

1. Accessibility and Convenience

Digital platforms have revolutionized investment by making it more accessible and convenient. Online trading platforms, mobile apps, and robo-advisors allow investors to manage their investments and execute trades from anywhere.

a. Lower Barriers to Entry

The accessibility of digital platforms lowers the barriers to entry for new investors, enabling them to start investing with minimal capital. This democratization of investment opportunities has expanded the participation of the Indian middle class in financial markets.

b. Real-Time Information

Digital platforms provide real-time information on market trends, financial news, and investment performance. This instant access to information helps investors make timely decisions and stay informed about their investments.

2. Robo-Advisors

a. Automated Investment Management

Robo-advisors use algorithms to offer automated investment management services. They provide portfolio recommendations based on an investor's risk profile and financial goals, often at lower costs compared to traditional advisors.

b. Accessibility for Small Investors

Robo-advisors democratize investment management by offering services with lower minimum investment requirements. This innovation has broadened access to professional investment management for smaller investors.

Influence of Social Media

1. Information and Trends

a. Financial Influencers

Social media platforms host a wide range of financial influencers who share investment tips, market analyses, and personal experiences. These influencers can shape investor perceptions and behavior by providing insights and recommendations.

b. Investment Communities

Online investment communities and forums allow individuals to discuss investment strategies, share knowledge, and seek advice from peers. These platforms can enhance financial literacy but may also contribute to herd behavior and misinformation.

2. Risks and Challenges

a. Misinformation

Social media can propagate misinformation and speculative advice, which may mislead investors. It is crucial for individuals to critically evaluate the credibility of information and avoid making investment decisions based solely on social media trends.

b. Herd Behavior

Social media can amplify herd behavior, where individuals follow the crowd rather than making decisions based on their own analysis. This behavior can lead to market bubbles and increased volatility.

Conclusion

Education and financial literacy are fundamental to making informed investment decisions. Access to education, effective financial literacy programs, and the role of financial advisors contribute to better investment outcomes. Additionally, digital platforms and social media play significant roles in shaping investment behavior. By enhancing financial education and leveraging technological advancements, the Indian middle class can navigate the complexities of modern investing more effectively.

❖ ❖ ❖

CHAPTER 5: THE IMPACT OF GOVERNMENT POLICIES ON INVESTMENT DECISIONS

Introduction

Government policies, regulations, and economic reforms are pivotal in shaping the investment landscape of any country. In India, these factors have had a profound impact on the investment behavior of the middle class, a demographic that plays a crucial role in the nation's economy. This chapter explores how tax incentives, subsidies, and regulatory frameworks influence investment decisions. Additionally, it delves into the effects of major economic policies such as demonetization and the introduction of the Goods and Services Tax (GST) on the investment patterns of the Indian middle class.

1. **Tax Incentives and Investment Behavior**

    a. **Tax-Exempt Investments**

    Tax incentives are one of the most powerful tools the government uses to influence investment behavior. Tax-exempt investments, such as those under Section 80C of the Income Tax Act, have been instrumental in shaping the portfolio choices of the Indian middle class.

    Overview: Section 80C allows deductions of up to ₹1.5 lakh per annum on investments in specified financial instruments such as Public Provident Fund (PPF), Employee Provident Fund (EPF), National Savings Certificates (NSC), and Equity-Linked Savings Schemes (ELSS).

    Impact: These tax benefits have traditionally driven middle-class households to prioritize safe, government-backed savings schemes, thus promoting a culture of savings over consumption. The availability of tax deductions has also encouraged long-term financial planning.

b. Taxation on Capital Gains

The taxation of capital gains (profits earned from the sale of financial assets such as stocks, bonds, or real estate) also significantly influences investment decisions. The introduction of the Long-Term Capital Gains (LTCG) tax on equity investments in 2018 marked a notable shift in the tax landscape.

Overview: The LTCG tax imposes a 10% tax on gains exceeding ₹1 lakh from equity investments held for more than one year.

Impact: The introduction of LTCG tax has made investors more cautious, leading to a preference for alternative investment avenues that offer similar returns with potentially lower tax implications.

2. Subsidies and Their Influence on Investment Choices

a. Housing Subsidies and Real Estate Investments

Housing subsidies, particularly those provided under the Pradhan Mantri Awas Yojana (PMAY), have had a significant impact on the real estate investment decisions of the middle class. These subsidies make home ownership more accessible and attractive.

Overview: PMAY provides interest subsidies on home loans for individuals in the Economically Weaker Section (EWS) and Low-Income Group (LIG).

Impact: These subsidies have boosted demand for affordable housing, encouraging the middle class to invest in real estate as a stable and appreciating asset.

b. Agricultural Subsidies and Rural Investment

Agricultural subsidies, including those for fertilizers, seeds, and electricity, indirectly impact the investment patterns of the rural middle class. These subsidies increase disposable income in rural areas, some of which is directed towards savings and investments.

Overview: The government provides various subsidies to the agricultural sector, aiming to reduce costs and improve profitability.

Impact: With increased disposable income, rural households have more funds available for investment, leading to greater participation in financial markets and traditional savings instruments.

3. Regulatory Frameworks and Market Access

a. Securities Market Regulations

Regulations introduced by the Securities and Exchange Board of India (SEBI) have had a profound effect on market transparency and investor protection. These regulations have bolstered investor confidence and expanded market participation.

Overview: SEBI's regulations on insider trading, corporate governance, and mutual funds ensure fair practices and protect investor interests.

Impact: Enhanced transparency and reduced market manipulation have encouraged more middle-class investors to participate in the equity markets.

b. The Role of Pension Reforms

Pension reforms, particularly the introduction of the National Pension System (NPS), have provided the middle class with new avenues for retirement savings. The NPS offers a flexible and regulated retirement savings option, which has gained popularity among the middle class.

Overview: The NPS allows individuals to contribute to a pension account during their working life, with the accumulated corpus being used to purchase an annuity upon retirement.

Impact: NPS has encouraged long-term savings by offering tax benefits and flexibility in investment choices, making it an attractive option for retirement planning.

4. **Economic Reforms and Their Impact on Investment Patterns**

   a. **Demonetization and Its Aftermath**

   The demonetization of ₹500 and ₹1,000 currency notes in 2016 was a landmark economic reform that had far-reaching effects on the investment behavior of the Indian middle class. The sudden withdrawal of these high-denomination notes disrupted the economy and led to a shift towards digital transactions and formal banking channels.

   Overview: Demonetization aimed to curb black money, counterfeit currency, and promote a digital economy.

   Impact: The immediate impact was a surge in deposits into banks, followed by increased investments in mutual funds and digital financial instruments as cash transactions declined.

   b. **Introduction of the Goods and Services Tax (GST)**

   The introduction of the Goods and Services Tax (GST) in 2017 was another significant reform that affected the investment landscape. GST replaced multiple indirect taxes with a unified tax structure, simplifying the tax system and reducing compliance costs.

   Overview: GST is a comprehensive, multi-stage, destination-based tax that is levied on every value addition.

   Impact: By reducing the tax burden and streamlining tax administration, GST has increased disposable income, encouraging more investments in financial markets and real estate.

Conclusion

Government policies, including tax incentives, subsidies, and regulatory frameworks, have a profound impact on the investment decisions of the Indian middle class. Economic reforms such as demonetization and the introduction of GST have further reshaped the investment landscape, influencing how the middle class allocates its resources. As the government continues to introduce new policies and reforms, their impact on investment behavior will remain a critical area of study. Understanding these dynamics is essential for predicting future trends and guiding the middle class in making informed investment decisions.

CHAPTER 6: REAL ESTATE: A FAVOURED BUT RISKY BET

Introduction

In India, real estate has long been regarded as the ultimate investment goal for many in the middle class. The appeal of owning property is deeply embedded in cultural values, symbolizing not only financial security but also social status and personal achievement. However, real estate investment is fraught with risks and challenges. This chapter examines the allure of property investment, the risks associated with it, and the various challenges posed by market fluctuations, regulatory hurdles, and the issue of affordable housing. Additionally, it explores the emotional and cultural significance of property ownership in India.

1. The Allure of Real Estate Investment

a. Cultural and Emotional Significance

In India, property ownership carries significant cultural weight. It is often seen as a mark of success and stability, intertwined with family values and social status. Owning a home is perceived as a key milestone in personal and financial life, often associated with a sense of security and accomplishment.

Cultural Context: Property ownership is often seen as a necessary step towards establishing a secure future, particularly for those in the middle class. This sentiment is amplified by the importance placed on leaving behind a legacy for future generations.

b. Financial Perceptions

Real estate is often viewed as a tangible and stable asset that appreciates over time, providing both financial security and potential for wealth accumulation. For many middle-class families, the decision to invest in property is driven by the belief that it is a low-risk investment that can offer significant returns, especially in urban areas.

Economic Context: Historically, property values in urban areas have shown consistent appreciation, making real estate a favoured option for long-term investment. This perception is strengthened by the lack of comprehensive financial education that highlights the risks associated with real estate.

2. The Risks of Real Estate Investment

a. Market Volatility

Real estate markets in India are subject to fluctuations based on various factors including economic conditions, interest rates, and regional developments. These fluctuations can lead to significant risks for investors.

Market Trends: Property prices can vary widely between different cities and regions. Economic downturns or shifts in demand can lead to decreased property values, affecting investment returns.

b. Regulatory Hurdles

Navigating the regulatory environment in India can be challenging for real estate investors. Issues such as complex property laws, delays in approvals, and the lack of transparency can pose significant risks.

Regulatory Challenges: Problems such as unclear property titles, slow legal processes, and bureaucratic inefficiencies can lead to delays and additional costs. The implementation of the Real Estate (Regulation and Development) Act (RERA) has aimed to address some of these issues, but challenges remain.

c. Liquidity Concerns

Real estate is relatively illiquid compared to other forms of investment such as stocks or mutual funds. Selling property can be a lengthy process, and market conditions may force investors to sell at a lower price.

Liquidity Risks: The process of buying and selling property involves significant time and transaction costs. The lack of liquidity can be a significant drawback for investors who may need quick access to cash. In such situations, property investments can become a financial burden rather than an asset.

3. Challenges in Affordable Housing

a. Urbanization and Housing Demand

The rapid urbanization of India has led to a surge in demand for housing, particularly in major cities. However, the supply of affordable housing has not kept pace with demand, leading to inflated property prices and making homeownership increasingly difficult for the middle class.

Lack of Supply: The high cost of urban housing has led many middle-class families to invest in properties located in the outskirts or in smaller cities, where prices are more affordable. However, these investments come with their own set of risks, including lower appreciation rates and potential infrastructure deficits.

b. Government Initiatives

The Indian government has implemented various schemes to promote affordable housing, including subsidies and incentives for developers and buyers. These initiatives are designed to make housing more accessible to the middle class.

Policy Impact: While these policies have had some success in increasing housing availability, issues such as bureaucratic delays and ineffective implementation often hinder their effectiveness. Ensuring that these initiatives reach the intended beneficiaries remains a challenge.

4. Emotional and Cultural Significance of Property Ownership

a. Real Estate as a Status Symbol

Property ownership in India is not just a financial investment but also a status symbol. The aspiration to own property is often linked to social status and personal success, reflecting broader cultural values.

Societal Impact: The cultural emphasis on property ownership can lead to over-leveraging, where individuals may take on significant debt to achieve home ownership. This can create financial strain and impact long-term financial stability.

b. Generational Perspectives on Real Estate

The value placed on property ownership is often passed down through generations, reinforcing its importance within families. This generational perspective shapes investment choices and financial priorities.

Family Legacy: For many families, property ownership

is seen as a way to secure a legacy and provide stability for future generations. This perspective can influence investment decisions and financial planning.

Conclusion

Real estate remains a favoured investment for the Indian middle class, driven by cultural values, perceived financial security, and social status. However, the risks associated with real estate investment, including market volatility, regulatory challenges, and liquidity concerns, must be carefully considered. Additionally, the issue of affordable housing continues to pose significant challenges, despite government efforts to address the gap. Understanding these factors is crucial for making informed investment decisions and balancing the cultural and financial aspects of property ownership.

CHAPTER 7: THE RISE OF MUTUAL FUNDS AND STOCK MARKETS IN INDIA

Introduction

In recent years, the Indian stock market and mutual funds have witnessed unprecedented growth, particularly among the middle class. This trend has been driven by a combination of factors, including increased financial literacy, the rise of digital investment platforms, and the quest for higher returns in a low-interest-rate environment. As these markets continue to evolve, they offer both opportunities and challenges for individual investors. This chapter delves into the factors contributing to this phenomenon and highlights the associated risks and the importance of a diversified investment approach.

Historical Context: The Evolution of Stock Markets and Mutual Funds in India

The Indian stock market has a long history, with the Bombay Stock Exchange (BSE) established in 1875 as Asia's first stock exchange. However, for much of its history, stock market participation was largely confined to institutional investors and a small segment of wealthy individuals. The liberalization of India's economy in the early 1990s marked a significant shift, with reforms aimed at enhancing market transparency, fostering competition, and opening up the market to foreign investors. These reforms led to a modernization of the financial sector and a gradual increase in retail participation.

Mutual funds, on the other hand, were first introduced in India in 1963 with the establishment of the Unit Trust of India (UTI). For several decades, UTI was the sole player in the market, offering a limited range of schemes. The entry of private sector mutual funds in the 1990s, followed by regulatory reforms by the Securities and Exchange Board of India (SEBI), transformed the mutual fund landscape. These reforms ensured greater transparency, better governance, and a more investor-friendly environment, contributing to the steady growth of the industry.

Factors Driving the Growth of Mutual Funds and Stock Market Participation

1. Financial Education Campaigns

Financial literacy plays a crucial role in increasing participation in mutual funds and stock markets. SEBI, the Reserve Bank of India (RBI), and the Association of Mutual Funds in India (AMFI) have all launched various initiatives aimed at educating the public on financial matters. Campaigns like "Mutual Funds Sahi Hai," spearheaded by AMFI, have been particularly successful in making mutual funds accessible to the average investor by simplifying complex financial concepts. These initiatives have led to a better understanding of the benefits and risks associated with mutual funds and stock market investments, thereby boosting confidence among retail investors.

2. Digital Platforms and Market Access

The advent of digital technology has revolutionized the way Indians invest. Online trading platforms and mobile applications have made it easier than ever for individuals to access the stock market and invest in mutual funds. New age companies have democratized investing by offering low-cost, user-friendly platforms that cater to a wide audience, including first-time investors. The convenience of digital transactions, combined with the ability to track and manage investments in real time, has significantly lowered the barriers to entry and attracted a large number of middle-class investors.

3. Search for Higher Returns in a Low-Interest-Rate Environment

The low-interest-rate environment in recent years has also played a crucial role in driving middle-class investors toward mutual funds and stock markets. Traditional savings instruments like fixed deposits and savings accounts have offered diminishing returns, prompting investors to seek alternatives that can potentially yield higher returns. Equity mutual funds, in particular, have become an attractive option for those looking to grow their wealth over the long term. The awareness that equities have the potential to outperform other asset classes over extended periods has led to a shift in the investment mindset of the middle class.

Risks Associated with Equity Investments

While the potential for higher returns in the stock market is appealing, equity investments come with their own set of risks. The volatility of stock markets, driven by factors such as economic fluctuations, political instability, and global events, can lead to substantial losses. Additionally, behavioural biases such as overconfidence, herd mentality, and loss aversion can negatively impact investment decisions.

1. Market Volatility

Stock markets are inherently volatile, with prices subject to rapid changes due to various factors, including macroeconomic indicators, corporate performance, and global events. For instance, the COVID-19 pandemic led to significant market turbulence, causing substantial losses for many investors. Understanding and accepting the nature of market volatility is crucial for investors to avoid making impulsive decisions during market downturns.

2. Behavioral Biases

Behavioral biases can lead to irrational investment decisions. For example, during a bull market, investors may become overconfident and take on excessive risk, while in a bear market, they may panic and sell off assets at a loss. Recognizing these biases and maintaining a disciplined investment approach is essential for long-term success in the stock market.

3. Lack of Diversification

Investing in a single stock or sector increases the risk

of significant losses if that investment underperforms. Diversification, both within and across asset classes, is a fundamental strategy for managing risk. Mutual funds inherently provide diversification by pooling investments across a wide range of assets, but investors must still choose funds that align with their risk tolerance and investment goals.

Importance of a Diversified Portfolio

To mitigate the risks associated with equity investments, it is essential for investors to maintain a diversified portfolio. Diversification helps spread risk across various asset classes, sectors, and geographies, reducing the impact of any single investment's poor performance on the overall portfolio. For middle-class investors, a well-diversified portfolio might include a mix of equity mutual funds, debt instruments, gold, and real estate. The specific allocation would depend on the individual's risk tolerance, investment horizon, and financial goals.

Mutual funds, by their nature, offer a level of diversification that is difficult to achieve through direct stock investments, especially for small investors. There are various types of mutual funds available, including equity funds, debt funds, hybrid funds, and index funds, each catering to different risk appetites and investment objectives. The key is to choose a combination of funds that aligns with one's financial goals while providing a balance between risk and return.

Conclusion

The rise of mutual funds and stock market participation among the Indian middle class is a testament to the increasing financial awareness and the search for better investment opportunities. While the potential for higher returns in equity markets is attractive, it comes with its own set of risks. Understanding these risks, staying informed, and maintaining a diversified portfolio are critical for investors looking to build wealth over the long term. As the financial landscape continues to evolve, the Indian middle class will likely play an increasingly significant role in shaping the future of the country's capital markets.

CHAPTER 8: GOLD: THE TRADITIONAL SAFE HAVEN

Introduction

For centuries, gold has occupied a special place in Indian society, symbolizing wealth, prosperity, and security. Despite the rise of various modern investment avenues, gold continues to hold significant appeal for the Indian middle class. This chapter explores the deep-rooted cultural and historical reasons behind India's enduring fascination with gold, examining how it has maintained its position as a preferred investment. The chapter also evaluates the pros and cons of investing in gold in today's economic environment, offering a balanced perspective for investors.

Historical and Cultural Significance of Gold in India

The relationship between gold and Indian society dates back thousands of years. Historically, gold has been associated with wealth, power, and divinity. Ancient Indian texts, including the Vedas and Puranas, extol the virtues of gold, often linking it to gods and goddesses. Gold ornaments have been discovered in archaeological sites dating back to the Indus Valley Civilization, highlighting its early use and significance in Indian culture.

Gold's importance is deeply ingrained in Indian traditions and rituals. It plays a central role in religious ceremonies, festivals, and life events such as weddings. Reflecting the belief that gold symbolizes financial security and social status. Festivals like Akshaya Tritiya and Dhanteras are considered auspicious for buying gold, reinforcing its cultural significance.

For the Indian middle class, gold has historically served as both a status symbol and a form of financial security. In times of economic instability, gold is seen as a stable asset that can preserve wealth across generations. This belief is rooted in centuries of experience, where gold has consistently proven to be a reliable store of value, particularly during periods of political upheaval, inflation, or currency devaluation.

The Modern Context: Gold as an Investment

In the modern era, the investment landscape in India has diversified significantly, with the rise of stocks, mutual funds, real estate, and other financial instruments. However, gold remains a popular choice, particularly among the middle class. Several factors contribute to the continued appeal of gold as an investment in contemporary India.

1. Inflation Hedge

Gold is widely regarded as a hedge against inflation. When inflation rises, the purchasing power of currency decreases, leading investors to seek assets that can preserve their wealth. Historically, gold prices have tended to rise during periods of high inflation, making it an attractive option for those looking to protect their savings from the eroding effects of rising prices. This is particularly relevant in India, where inflation has been a recurring concern.

2. Diversification of Portfolio

For modern investors, diversification is a key strategy for managing risk. Gold is often included in investment portfolios as a diversification tool because its price movements tend to be uncorrelated with those of other asset classes like stocks and bonds. During times of market volatility or economic downturns, gold often performs well, providing a safety net for investors. This characteristic makes gold a valuable component of a balanced investment portfolio.

3. Liquidity and Accessibility

One of the advantages of gold as an investment is its high liquidity. Gold can be easily bought and sold in the market, making it a flexible asset for investors. Moreover, in India, gold is available in various forms, including jewellery, coins, bars, and financial products like Gold ETFs (Exchange Traded Funds) and Sovereign Gold Bonds. This accessibility ensures that investors from different economic backgrounds can participate in gold investment according to their financial capacity.

4. Cultural and Emotional Attachment

Despite the availability of other investment options, the cultural and emotional attachment to gold remains strong in India. Gold is not just seen as a financial asset; it is also valued for its aesthetic appeal and cultural significance. For many Indian families, gold jewelry serves a dual purpose—both as an investment and as a symbol of tradition and heritage. This cultural attachment reinforces the demand for gold, particularly during festivals and weddings.

Pros and Cons of Investing in Gold

While gold has been a trusted investment for generations, it is important to evaluate its pros and cons in the context of modern financial planning.

Pros:

1. Stability and Security

Gold has a long history of being a stable and secure investment. Unlike other assets that may be affected by market fluctuations or economic downturns, gold typically retains its value, making it a reliable store of wealth over time.

2. Inflation Protection

As an inflation hedge, gold is unmatched. It has consistently maintained its purchasing power even during periods of high inflation, making it an essential component of any investment strategy aimed at preserving wealth.

3. Liquidity

The high liquidity of gold allows investors to quickly convert their assets into cash when needed. This flexibility is especially important in times of financial emergency, where access to funds is crucial.

4. Cultural Significance

The cultural importance of gold in India ensures a steady demand for the metal. This intrinsic value, tied to tradition and social practices, provides an additional layer of security for investors.

Cons:

1. No Yield

Unlike stocks or bonds, gold does not generate any income. There are no dividends or interest payments associated with gold, which means that investors do not benefit from any cash flow while holding the asset. This can be a disadvantage for those seeking regular income from their investments.

2. Storage and Security Costs

Physical gold requires secure storage, which can be costly. Whether stored at home or in a bank, the need for security can add to the overall cost of holding gold, reducing the net returns from the investment.

3. Price Volatility

While gold is considered a stable investment over the long term, its price can be volatile in the short term. Global economic factors, changes in demand, and shifts in investor sentiment can lead to significant price fluctuations, posing a risk for short-term investors.

4. Opportunity Cost

Investing heavily in gold may mean missing out on higher returns from other asset classes, such as equities. While gold provides security, it may not offer the same growth potential as other investments, leading to opportunity costs for investors focused on long-term wealth accumulation.

Conclusion

Gold's enduring appeal in India is rooted in a combination of cultural, historical, and economic factors. For the Indian middle class, gold represents more than just a financial investment; it embodies wealth, security, and tradition. While modern investment options have diversified the avenues available to investors, gold continues to play a crucial role in financial planning, particularly as a hedge against inflation and a tool for portfolio diversification.

However, as with any investment, it is important to weigh the pros and cons of investing in gold. While it offers safety and liquidity, it lacks the income potential of other investments and can be costly to store. A balanced approach that includes gold as part of a diversified portfolio may be the most prudent strategy for investors seeking both stability and growth in their financial journey.

CHAPTER 9: THE CHALLENGE OF RETIREMENT PLANNING

Introduction

Retirement planning is a critical aspect of financial management that is often overlooked, especially within the Indian middle class. With the absence of a comprehensive social security system, the responsibility of ensuring financial security in retirement largely falls on individuals. The challenge is further compounded by the need to balance current expenses with future financial needs. This chapter delves into the importance of long-term financial planning, the role of pension schemes, and the unique challenges faced by the Indian middle class in preparing for retirement.

The Importance of Long-Term Financial Planning

In India, where life expectancy has been steadily increasing, the need for robust retirement planning has become more pressing. As individuals live longer, the risk of outliving one's savings becomes a significant concern. Long-term financial planning is essential to mitigate this risk and ensure a stable and secure retirement.

1. **Financial Independence in Old Age**

   The primary goal of retirement planning is to achieve financial independence in old age. This involves accumulating sufficient savings and investments during one's working years to cover living expenses, healthcare costs, and other needs in retirement. Without adequate planning, individuals may find themselves financially dependent on family members, which can strain relationships and reduce quality of life.

2. **Inflation and Its Impact**

Inflation is a critical factor to consider in retirement planning. The cost of living continues to rise, eroding the purchasing power of money over time. What might seem like an adequate retirement corpus today could prove insufficient in the future if inflation is not accounted for. Effective retirement planning requires strategies that not only grow savings but also protect them against the eroding effects of inflation.

3. Healthcare Costs

Healthcare costs are a significant concern for retirees, often increasing with age. The rising cost of healthcare in India, combined with the limited scope of health insurance coverage, makes it essential to plan for medical expenses as part of a comprehensive retirement plan. Failing to do so can lead to financial stress during retirement, especially if unexpected medical issues arise.

4. Evolving Social Dynamics

Traditionally, Indian families followed a joint family system where the younger generation took care of the elderly. However, with the shift towards nuclear families and the increasing mobility of the workforce, this support system is weakening. This change underscores the need for individual retirement planning, as relying on family support is no longer a viable option for many.

The Role of Pension Schemes in Retirement Planning

Pension schemes play a vital role in providing financial security during retirement. In India, the government and private sector offer various pension plans aimed at encouraging individuals to save for their retirement. Understanding these options is crucial for effective retirement planning.

1. Employee Provident Fund (EPF)

The Employee Provident Fund (EPF) is one of the most common retirement savings schemes in India. It is mandatory for salaried employees in organizations with more than 20 employees. Under the EPF scheme, both the employee and employer contribute a percentage of the employee's salary towards a retirement fund. The accumulated corpus, along with interest, is available to the employee upon retirement. While EPF provides a steady source of retirement income, it may not be sufficient to meet all retirement needs, especially given inflation and rising costs.

2. National Pension System (NPS)

The National Pension System (NPS) is a government-sponsored retirement savings scheme that is open to all Indian citizens. NPS offers flexibility in terms of investment options and fund management, allowing individuals to choose a mix of equity, corporate bonds, and government securities based on their risk appetite. The NPS is designed to provide a regular income after retirement, with a portion of the corpus available as a lump sum and the rest converted into an annuity. The NPS is gaining popularity due to its tax benefits and the potential for higher returns compared to traditional pension plans.

3. Atal Pension Yojana (APY)

The Atal Pension Yojana (APY) is a government-initiated pension scheme aimed at the unorganized sector. It offers a guaranteed minimum pension ranging from ₹1,000 to ₹5,000 per month, depending on the contribution amount. The scheme is designed to provide financial security to low-income individuals who may not have access to formal pension schemes. While APY is a step towards inclusive retirement planning, the benefits are modest and may not be sufficient to cover all retirement expenses.

4. Employer-Sponsored Pension Plans

In addition to government schemes, many employers in

India offer pension plans as part of their employee benefits package. These plans typically involve contributions from both the employer and the employee, with the accumulated funds being invested to generate returns. Employer-sponsored pension plans can provide a significant boost to retirement savings, but their availability is largely limited to the organized sector.

Challenges Faced by the Indian Middle Class in Retirement Planning

Despite the availability of various pension schemes, the Indian middle class faces several challenges in retirement planning. These challenges stem from economic, social, and behavioural factors that make it difficult for individuals to save adequately for their retirement.

1. Balancing Current Expenses with Future Needs

One of the most significant challenges in retirement planning is balancing current expenses with future needs. The Indian middle class often faces financial pressures such as home loans, children's education, and day-to-day living expenses, which can make it difficult to allocate funds towards retirement savings. The tendency to prioritize immediate financial needs over long-term planning can lead to insufficient retirement savings.

2. Low Financial Literacy

Financial literacy is crucial for effective retirement planning, yet many Indians lack a deep understanding of financial products and strategies. This lack of knowledge can lead to poor investment choices, underestimating retirement needs, and an over-reliance on suboptimal savings instruments. Enhancing financial literacy through education and awareness programs is essential to help individuals make informed decisions about their retirement planning.

3. Inadequate Pension Coverage

Despite the existence of various pension schemes, a significant portion of the Indian population remains outside the formal pension system. This is particularly true for those working in the unorganized sector, which constitutes a large part of the Indian workforce. Without access to formal pension plans, these individuals are at risk of financial insecurity in old age.

4. Cultural Attitudes Towards Retirement

Cultural attitudes and societal norms also play a role in shaping retirement planning behavior. In India, there is a strong cultural emphasis on family support during old age, which can lead to a reliance on children for financial security. However, with changing family dynamics and increased mobility, this reliance may not be feasible in the future. Encouraging a shift in mindset towards self-reliance and proactive retirement planning is crucial.

5. Inflation and Rising Costs

Inflation poses a significant challenge to retirement planning, as it erodes the value of savings over time. The rising cost of living, particularly in urban areas, means that individuals need to save more to maintain their standard of living in retirement. However, many individuals underestimate the impact of inflation on their retirement corpus, leading to insufficient savings.

6. Healthcare Costs

With advances in medical technology and increased life expectancy, healthcare costs have risen sharply, especially for retirees. Unfortunately, many retirement plans do not adequately account for these costs, leading to financial strain when medical needs arise. Comprehensive health insurance and dedicated medical funds are necessary components of any retirement plan to mitigate this risk.

Conclusion

Retirement planning is a complex and multifaceted challenge for the Indian middle class, requiring careful consideration of various factors, including inflation, healthcare costs, and changing social dynamics. The absence of a comprehensive social security system in India places the onus on individuals to secure their financial future. While pension schemes like the EPF, NPS, and APY provide some support, they are often insufficient on their own.

Addressing the challenges of retirement planning requires a combination of increased financial literacy, proactive long-term planning, and a shift in cultural attitudes towards self-reliance in old age. By recognizing the importance of retirement planning and taking early steps to build a robust financial strategy, individuals can ensure a secure and dignified retirement.

CHAPTER 10: THE ROLE OF TECHNOLOGY AND DIGITAL PLATFORMS

Introduction

The rapid advancement of technology has brought about a significant transformation in the investment landscape in India. Over the past decade, digital platforms, mobile applications, and robo-advisors have revolutionized the way individuals approach investing, particularly among the middle class. These tools have democratized access to financial markets, offering convenience, transparency, and a range of investment options at the click of a button. However, with these advancements come new challenges, including the potential for fraud and the critical importance of cybersecurity. This chapter explores the role of technology in reshaping investments in India, discussing both its benefits and associated risks.

The Emergence of Digital Platforms

1. Accessibility and Convenience

The most significant impact of digital platforms on investing is the enhanced accessibility they provide. Traditionally, investing in stocks, mutual funds, or other financial instruments required intermediaries like brokers, who often charged high fees and provided limited transparency. Today, digital platforms have eliminated many of these barriers, allowing individuals to invest directly through user-friendly interfaces available on smartphones and computers.

New-age Investing have gained popularity by offering a seamless, hassle-free experience where users can open accounts, conduct transactions, and monitor their portfolios with ease. These platforms have been particularly attractive to the Indian middle class, who may have previously found the traditional investing process intimidating or inaccessible.

2. Cost-Effectiveness

Digital platforms have also contributed to making investing more cost-effective. By reducing or eliminating brokerage fees and providing direct market access, these platforms have lowered the cost of investing, making it more feasible for a broader range of investors. For the middle class, this reduction in costs is significant, as it allows more of their investment capital to be allocated to the markets rather than being eroded by fees.

3. Robo-Advisors and Automated Investment Services

Robo-advisors have introduced a new dimension to investing by providing automated, algorithm-driven financial planning services with minimal human intervention. These services typically assess an individual's risk tolerance, financial goals, and time horizon before recommending a diversified portfolio of assets. Robo-advisors have become popular in India, especially among younger investors who prefer a low-cost, automated approach to managing their finances.

The use of robo-advisors is particularly appealing to those with limited financial knowledge or time to manage their investments actively. By automating the investment process, these platforms offer a convenient and accessible way to participate in the markets, while also helping to mitigate the emotional biases that can often negatively impact investment decisions.

Benefits of Technology-Driven Investment Platforms

1. Increased Financial Literacy

One of the indirect benefits of digital platforms is the increase in financial literacy among users. Many platforms offer educational resources, tutorials, and market insights that help investors understand the complexities of financial markets. This increased knowledge empowers individuals to make informed investment decisions, leading to better financial outcomes.

2. Transparency and Control

Digital platforms provide investors with greater transparency and control over their investments. Users can track the performance of their portfolios in real-time, access detailed reports, and make adjustments as needed. This level of transparency builds trust and encourages more proactive management of personal finances.

3. Diversification

Technology has made it easier for investors to diversify their portfolios across a range of asset classes, including equities, bonds, mutual funds, and even international markets. Platforms often provide tools and recommendations for building diversified portfolios, reducing the risk associated with concentrated investments.

4. Tailored Investment Solutions

With the help of big data and machine learning, digital platforms can offer personalized investment recommendations based on an individual's financial profile. These tailored solutions help investors align their portfolios with their specific goals, risk tolerance, and time horizon, leading to more effective financial planning.

Risks Associated with Technology in Investing

1. Cybersecurity Threats

As more financial activities move online, the risk of cyber threats increases. Digital platforms are prime targets for cybercriminals seeking to steal personal information, financial data, or even siphon off funds from user accounts. The Indian investment landscape has seen instances of data breaches and cyberattacks, highlighting the critical need for robust cybersecurity measures.

To mitigate these risks, investors must choose platforms that prioritize security, such as those that offer two-factor authentication, encryption, and regular security audits. Additionally, users should practice good cybersecurity hygiene, such as using strong passwords and being cautious of phishing attempts.

2. Potential for Fraud

The ease of access provided by digital platforms also opens the door to potential fraud. Scammers can create fake investment platforms or schemes that appear legitimate, luring unsuspecting investors into fraudulent activities. The Indian market has witnessed cases of Ponzi schemes and other fraudulent investment schemes conducted through online platforms.

To protect themselves, investors must conduct thorough due diligence before committing to any platform or investment. This includes checking the platform's registration with regulatory bodies like the Securities and Exchange Board of India (SEBI) and reading reviews or feedback from other users.

3. Over-Reliance on Technology

While technology has made investing more accessible, it can also lead to an over-reliance on automated systems and algorithms. This dependency can be risky if investors do not fully understand the underlying strategies or if the algorithms fail to adapt to market conditions. Moreover, during periods of high market volatility, automated systems may not always perform optimally, potentially leading to significant losses.

4. Market Volatility and Emotional Investing

The convenience of digital platforms means that investors can make trades at any time, but this also increases the temptation to react emotionally to short-term market movements. Frequent trading driven by fear or greed can result in poor investment decisions and lower overall returns. It is essential for investors to maintain a disciplined approach and not let the ease of trading lead to impulsive decisions.

The Future of Technology in Investing

The role of technology in the Indian investment landscape is likely to continue expanding, with further innovations on the horizon. The integration of artificial intelligence (AI), blockchain, and other advanced technologies promises to enhance the efficiency, security, and accessibility of investment platforms. For instance, AI-driven predictive analytics could offer even more personalized investment advice, while blockchain could provide enhanced security and transparency in transactions.

However, with these advancements come new challenges, particularly in terms of regulation and cybersecurity. As technology evolves, so too must the regulatory frameworks that govern the financial industry. Ensuring that these innovations are used responsibly and securely will be key to maintaining investor trust and safeguarding financial markets.

Conclusion

The role of technology and digital platforms in the Indian investment landscape cannot be overstated. These advancements have made investing more accessible, affordable, and efficient, particularly for the middle class. However, with these benefits come certain risks, including cybersecurity threats, fraud, and the limitations of automated investing.

To fully harness the potential of digital investment platforms, it is essential for investors to be aware of these risks and take proactive steps to mitigate them. This includes adopting robust cybersecurity practices, enhancing digital literacy, and seeking professional advice when necessary. As the investment landscape continues to evolve, a balanced approach that leverages the benefits of technology while addressing its challenges will be key to ensuring the financial well-being of the Indian middle class.

CHAPTER 11: WOMEN AND INVESTMENT: A GROWING INFLUENCE

Introduction

In recent years, the landscape of financial decision-making in India has witnessed a significant shift, with women emerging as key players in the realm of investments. As more women achieve financial independence, they are increasingly taking charge of their finances, challenging traditional gender norms, and contributing to the economic growth of the middle class. This chapter delves into the unique challenges and opportunities faced by women in the Indian middle class, exploring the impact of gender norms, the growing importance of financial education, and the rise of women-specific investment products.

The Influence of Gender Norms on Investment Decisions

1. Traditional Gender Roles and Financial Dependency

Traditionally, Indian society has placed the responsibility of financial decision-making on men, while women were expected to manage household duties. This division of roles often left women financially dependent on their male counterparts, limiting their exposure to investment opportunities. Despite the changing times, remnants of these gender norms persist, influencing how women approach financial decisions.

2. Evolving Social Dynamics

In recent years, there has been a significant shift in these dynamics. The increase in dual-income households, urbanization, and the rise of women in the workforce have all contributed to changing the traditional narrative. Women are now not only contributing financially to their households but also taking on active roles in investment decisions. This shift is particularly evident in the Indian middle class, where women are becoming more financially aware and empowered to make investment decisions.

The Growing Importance of Financial Education for Women

1. The Financial Literacy Gap

Financial literacy is a critical factor in empowering women to make informed investment decisions. However, studies indicate that women in India are generally less financially literate than men. This gap can be attributed to historical exclusion from financial decision-making, lower levels of formal education in some regions, and a lack of targeted financial education programs for women.

2. Initiatives to Improve Financial Literacy

Recognizing the importance of financial literacy, various initiatives have been launched to educate women about personal finance and investments. Organizations like SEBI (Securities and Exchange Board of India) and NISM (National Institute of Securities Markets) have developed programs aimed at increasing financial awareness among women. These programs cover essential topics such as budgeting, saving, investing, and retirement planning, providing women with the tools they need to manage their finances effectively.

3. The Role of Technology in Financial Education

The rise of digital platforms has made financial education more accessible to women across India. Online courses, webinars, and financial blogs are increasingly available, offering women the opportunity to learn at their own pace. Social media platforms also play a crucial role in spreading financial awareness, with many influencers and financial experts creating content specifically for women. These resources help women build confidence in their financial knowledge and empower them to take control of their investments.

The Rise of Women-Specific Investment Products

1. Understanding Women's Financial Needs

As more women take charge of their finances, the market has responded by developing women-specific investment products. These products are designed to address the unique financial goals and challenges faced by women, such as saving for children's education, planning for retirement, and ensuring financial security in case of life events like marriage or motherhood.

2. Examples of Women-Centric Financial Products

Several financial institutions in India have launched women-specific savings accounts, insurance policies, and mutual funds. For instance, certain banks offer savings accounts with higher interest rates and exclusive offers for women. Additionally, insurance companies have introduced health and life insurance policies that cater specifically to women's health concerns. Mutual fund companies have also started offering women-focused funds that invest in sectors aligned with women's financial goals, such as education, healthcare, and entrepreneurship.

3. Encouraging Women's Entrepreneurship

The rise of women-specific investment products is also linked to the growing trend of women's entrepreneurship in India. Women entrepreneurs often face unique challenges in accessing capital and financial resources. To address this, financial institutions have introduced loan schemes and investment products that support women-led businesses, encouraging more women to venture into entrepreneurship.

Challenges Faced by Women Investors

1. Cultural Barriers and Societal Expectations

Despite progress, women in India still face significant cultural barriers when it comes to investing. In many households, financial decisions are traditionally made by men, with women playing a secondary role. This can lead to a lack of confidence among women in making independent investment decisions. Overcoming these cultural barriers requires a shift in societal attitudes and increased support for women's financial empowerment.

2. Risk Aversion and Investment Behavior

Studies have shown that women tend to be more risk-averse than men when it comes to investing. This can lead to a preference for safer, lower-return investments, such as fixed deposits and savings accounts, over potentially higher-return options like equities and mutual funds. While risk aversion can be a prudent approach, it may also limit women's ability to achieve significant wealth creation over the long term. Overcoming this bias requires targeted financial education that emphasizes the importance of diversification and risk management.

3. Balancing Multiple Financial Goals

Women often face the challenge of balancing multiple financial goals, such as saving for children's education, managing household expenses, and planning for retirement. This can create a complex financial landscape where prioritizing investments becomes difficult. Financial advisors and digital platforms can play a key role in helping women navigate these challenges by offering personalized investment strategies that align with their diverse financial goals.

Opportunities for Women in the Investment Space

1. Leveraging Digital Platforms for Investment

Digital platforms have opened up new opportunities for women to take control of their investments. Mobile apps and online platforms provide women with easy access to a wide range of investment options, from mutual funds to equities, all from the convenience of their smartphones. These platforms also offer tools and resources to help women make informed decisions, track their portfolios, and adjust their strategies as needed.

2. Building Supportive Investment Communities

The rise of online investment communities has created a supportive environment for women to share knowledge, experiences, and advice. These communities, often found on social media or specialized financial forums, allow women to connect with others who are on similar financial journeys. By sharing their successes and challenges, women can learn from each other and build confidence in their investment decisions.

3. Promoting Women in Finance and Leadership Roles

Increasing the representation of women in finance and leadership roles is essential for driving gender diversity in the investment space. Women financial advisors, fund managers, and entrepreneurs serve as role models and mentors, inspiring more women to engage with their finances. Promoting gender diversity in the financial industry not only helps to break down barriers but also brings diverse perspectives to investment strategies and decision-making processes.

Conclusion

The role of women in investment decisions is evolving, driven by increasing financial independence, greater access to education, and the rise of women-specific financial products. While challenges such as cultural barriers, risk aversion, and the need to balance multiple financial goals persist, women are steadily carving out a larger space for themselves in the investment landscape. By leveraging the opportunities provided by digital platforms, building supportive investment communities, and promoting gender diversity in finance, women can continue to strengthen their influence in financial decision-making, ultimately contributing to their own financial security and the economic growth of the Indian middle class.

CHAPTER 12: THE FUTURE OF INVESTMENT IN INDIA

Introduction

The investment landscape in India is experiencing a transformative shift, influenced by evolving economic conditions, technological advancements, and changing social priorities. This chapter explores the future of investment for the Indian middle class, focusing on emerging trends such as sustainable investing, the impact of climate change on investment decisions, and the potential for new financial products and services. It also highlights the importance of continued financial education and the role of government policies in supporting the financial well-being of the middle class.

Emerging Trends in Investment

1. Sustainable Investing

a. Definition and Growth

Sustainable investing, or ESG (Environmental, Social, and Governance) investing, focuses on aligning investments with environmental and social values. It seeks to generate positive social and environmental impact alongside financial returns. In India, sustainable investing is gaining traction as investors become more conscious of the social and environmental implications of their investments. According to a report by the Global Sustainable Investment Alliance (GSIA), sustainable investment assets in India have seen a significant increase in recent years.

b. Key Drivers

The rise of sustainable investing in India is driven by

several factors:

Increased Awareness: Growing awareness about environmental issues, social justice, and corporate governance has led investors to seek out sustainable investment opportunities.

Regulatory Changes: Indian regulatory bodies, such as the Securities and Exchange Board of India (SEBI), are introducing guidelines to promote ESG disclosures and responsible investment practices.

Consumer Demand: Investors, especially younger generations, are demanding more ethical investment options that align with their values.

c. Investment Products

The growing interest in sustainable investing has led to the development of a variety of financial products. Green bonds, ESG-focused mutual funds, and socially responsible investment (SRI) funds are examples of products designed to meet the needs of investors who prioritize sustainability. These products support initiatives such as renewable energy projects, sustainable agriculture, and ethical corporate behavior.

2. Impact of Climate Change on Investment Decisions

a. Climate Risk and Investment Strategies

Climate change poses significant risks to investments, affecting sectors like real estate, agriculture, and energy. Investors are increasingly incorporating climate risk assessments into their investment strategies. This includes evaluating the potential impact of extreme weather events, regulatory changes related to carbon emissions, and shifts in consumer behavior towards more sustainable practices.

b. Climate Resilience

Investment strategies are evolving to include climate resilience as a key factor. This involves investing in industries and companies that are better equipped to handle climate related challenges, such as renewable energy, energy efficiency technologies, and sustainable infrastructure projects.

c. Government Initiatives

The Indian government is actively promoting climate-resilient investments through various policies and programs. The National Action Plan on Climate Change (NAPCC) and the promotion of green bonds are examples of initiatives aimed at encouraging investment in climate-friendly projects. These measures support the transition to a low-carbon economy and provide investors with opportunities to contribute to environmental sustainability.

3. Innovation in Financial Products and Services

a. Fintech Revolution

The fintech revolution is reshaping the investment landscape in India. Technological advancements are making financial services more accessible, efficient, and personalized. Innovations such as robo-advisors, mobile trading apps, and blockchain technology are transforming how investments are managed and executed.

b. New Financial Products

Financial institutions are introducing innovative products to meet the evolving needs of investors. These include fractional ownership of assets, peer-to-peer lending platforms, and investment solutions powered by artificial intelligence and machine learning. These new products offer greater flexibility and customization, allowing investors to tailor their portfolios to their specific goals and risk tolerance.

c. Digital Transformation

Digital transformation is enhancing the investment experience by providing investors with real-time data, automated investment solutions, and greater transparency. This shift is making it easier for individuals to manage their investments and make informed decisions.

The Importance of Continued Financial Education

1. Addressing the Financial Literacy Gap

As the investment landscape evolves, continued financial education is crucial for helping investors make informed decisions. Financial literacy programs need to address emerging trends such as sustainable investing and climate risk to ensure that investors are equipped with the knowledge to navigate these new challenges.

2. Empowering Investors

Financial education empowers individuals to take control of their financial futures. By understanding new investment products, market dynamics, and strategic planning, investors can make informed choices and optimize their investment outcomes. Educational initiatives should focus on providing practical knowledge and skills that are relevant to today's financial environment.

3. Role of Educational Institutions and Platforms

Educational institutions, financial advisors, and digital

platforms play a vital role in delivering financial education. Comprehensive training programs, online courses, and interactive tools can help investors stay up-to-date with the latest trends and strategies. Collaboration between these entities is essential for providing accessible and relevant financial education to a broad audience.

Government Policies and Support

1. Supporting Financial Well-being

Government policies play a vital role in shaping the investment environment and supporting the financial well-being of the middle class. Policies that promote financial inclusion, protect investor interests, and encourage responsible investing can help create a more stable and equitable financial system.

2. Regulatory Framework

A robust regulatory framework is essential for ensuring transparency and fairness in the investment market. The Indian government and regulatory bodies such as SEBI are working to update regulations to address emerging trends and challenges. This includes enhancing ESG disclosure requirements and supporting the development of sustainable investment products.

3. Incentives and Support Programs

The government can also support the investment community through incentives and support programs. This includes tax benefits for green investments, subsidies for renewable energy projects, and funding for financial literacy initiatives.

Conclusion

The future of investment in India is characterized by rapid change and innovation, driven by emerging trends such as sustainable investing, climate risk considerations, and technological advancements. As the Indian middle class continues to evolve, investors must stay informed and adaptable to navigate these changes successfully. Continued financial education and supportive government policies will play a crucial role in shaping a resilient and inclusive investment landscape. By embracing these trends and preparing for the future, investors can contribute to both their personal financial success and the broader economic and environmental well-being of the country.

Appendices

Appendix A: Glossary of Financial Terms

A

- **Assets:** Resources owned by an individual or business that have economic value.
- **Amortization:** The process of spreading out a loan into a series of fixed payments over time.
- **Annuity**: A financial product that provides a steady income stream, typically for retirees, in exchange for an initial investment.

B

- **Balance Sheet:** A financial statement that provides a snapshot of a company's financial condition at a specific moment in time.
- **Bonds:** Debt securities issued by corporations or governments to raise capital, with a promise to repay the principal along with interest.
- **Bullion**: Physical gold, silver, platinum, or palladium that is of high purity and typically in the form of bars or ingots.

C

- **Capital:** Wealth in the form of money or assets, used or accumulated in a business by a person, partnership, or corporation.
- **Capital Gains Tax**: A tax on the profit made from selling a property or investment.
- **Collateral:** An asset that a borrower offers to a lender to secure a loan.
- **Cryptocurrency**: A digital or virtual currency that uses cryptography for security and operates independently of a central bank.

D

- **Dividend:** A portion of a company's earnings distributed to shareholders.
- **Depreciation:** The decrease in the value of an asset over time.
- **Derivative:** A financial security whose value is dependent upon or derived from an underlying asset, such as gold futures.

E

- **Equity:** The value of an owner's interest in a company, calculated as the difference between assets and liabilities.
- **Exchange-Traded Fund (ETF):** A type of investment fund and exchange-traded product, traded on stock exchanges, much like stocks.
- **ETF (Exchange-Traded Fund):** A type of investment fund and exchange-traded product that invests in assets such as gold.

F

- **Fixed Income:** Investments that provide regular income, typically in the form of interest payments, like bonds.
- **Futures Contract:** A legal agreement to buy or sell a particular commodity asset, or security at a predetermined price at a specified time in the future.

G

- **Gross Domestic Product (GDP):** The total value of goods produced and services provided in a country during one year.
- **Growth Stocks:** Shares in a company that are anticipated to grow at a rate significantly above the average growth for the market.
- **Guaranteed Income:** A reliable source of income during retirement, often provided through annuities or pensions.

H

- **Hedge:** An investment to reduce the risk of adverse price movements in an asset, often used with gold to protect

against inflation.
- **Hedge Fund:** An investment fund that employs different strategies to earn active return for their investors.
- **High-Yield Bond:** A bond with a higher risk of default that provides a higher return to compensate for the risk.

I

- **Inflation:** The rate at which the general level of prices for goods and services is rising.
- **Index Fund:** A type of mutual fund with a portfolio constructed to match or track the components of a financial market index.
- **Intrinsic Value**: The perceived or calculated value of a gold coin or bar based on its gold content.
- **Inflation Risk**: The potential for inflation to erode the purchasing power of retirement savings over time.

J

- **Junk Bond:** A high-yield or non-investment grade bond with a lower credit rating and higher risk of default.

L

- **Liabilities:** A company's legal financial debts or obligations that arise during the course of business operations.
- **Liquidity:** The ability to quickly convert an asset into cash without a significant loss of value.
- **Life Expectancy**: The estimated number of years an individual is expected to live, often used to determine retirement planning needs.

M

- **Mutual Fund:** An investment program funded by shareholders that trades in diversified holdings and is professionally managed.
- **Margin:** Borrowing money from a broker to purchase stock, using other stocks in your portfolio as collateral.

N

- **Net Worth:** The total assets minus total liabilities of an individual or company.

O
- **NAV (Net Asset Value):** The value per share of a mutual fund or an ETF, calculated by dividing the total value of the fund's assets by the number of shares outstanding.

- **Option:** A financial derivative that represents a contract sold by one party to another, giving the buyer the right, but not the obligation, to buy or sell a security at an agreed-upon price during a certain period or on a specific date.

P
- **Portfolio:** A range of investments held by a person or organization.
- **Principal:** The original sum of money borrowed or invested, excluding any interest or dividends.
- **Premium**: The amount by which the price of gold exceeds its spot price, reflecting factors such as demand, supply, and market conditions.
- **Pension**: A retirement plan that provides a fixed, regular income to retirees, typically funded and managed by employers.
- **Portfolio Diversification**: The strategy of spreading investments across various asset classes to reduce risk.

R
- **Return on Investment (ROI):** A measure used to evaluate the efficiency of an investment or compare the efficiency of several investments.
- **Risk:** The potential for losing money on an investment or business venture.

S
- **Stock:** A share in the ownership of a company and represents a claim on part of the company's assets and earnings.
- **Securities:** Financial instruments that represent some type of financial value, such as stocks, bonds, or options.
- **Social Security**: A government program that provides financial benefits to retirees, disabled individuals, and

survivors of deceased workers.

T

- **Treasury Bills (T-Bills):** Short-term government securities with maturities ranging from a few days to 52 weeks.
- **Tax Deductible:** Expenses that can be subtracted from gross income to reduce taxable income.

V

- **Volatility:** A statistical measure of the dispersion of returns for a given security or market index.
- **Venture Capital:** Financing that investors provide to startup companies and small businesses that are believed to have long-term growth potential.
- **Virtual Currency:** A digital currency that exists only in electronic form and is not backed by a physical commodity.

Y

- **Yield:** The income return on an investment, such as the interest or dividends received from holding a particular security.

Appendix B: List of Investment Resources and Tools

Investment Resources

1. **HDFC Sky:** Provides detailed information on stocks, including fundamental and technical analyses, charts, news, and financials.
2. **NSE India:** The official website of the National Stock Exchange, offering financial information and stock quotes for all listed companies.
3. **BSE India:** The official website of the Bombay Stock Exchange, providing stock quotes and market data.
4. **Trade Brains Portal:** Offers stock market news, analysis, and investment strategies.
5. **Money Control:** A comprehensive financial website with

stock market data, news, and analysis.
6. **Screener**: A tool for screening stocks based on various criteria to find potential investment opportunities.
7. **Investing.com**: Provides global financial news, stock market data, and analysis tools.
8. **Economic Times Market**: Offers market news, stock analysis, and financial insights.

Investment Tools

1. **ET Money**: A personal finance app that helps with budgeting, expense tracking, and investment planning.
2. **Groww**: An investment platform that offers mutual funds, stocks, and ETFs with a user-friendly interface.
3. **Zerodha Coin**: A platform for trading cryptocurrencies with a focus on security and ease of use.
4. **Paytm Money**: Offers investment options in mutual funds, stocks, and insurance.
5. **Upstox**: A trading platform that provides tools for stock trading, derivatives, and currency trading.
6. **5Paisa**: A discount brokerage offering trading in stocks, commodities, and currency derivatives.
7. **Sharekhan**: A brokerage firm providing a range of investment services, including stocks, mutual funds, and derivatives.
8. **Motilal Oswal**: Offers investment services in stocks, mutual funds, and wealth management.
9. These resources and tools can help make informed investment decisions and manage portfolio effectively.

Appendix C: Government Schemes and Tax Benefits for Middle-Class Investors

Government Schemes

1. **Public Provident Fund (PPF)**: A long-term savings scheme with a lock-in period of 15 years, offering tax

benefits under Section 80C of the Income Tax Act.
2. **National Savings Certificate (NSC)**: A fixed-income investment scheme with a lock-in period of 5 years, also offering tax benefits under Section 80C.
3. **Sukanya Samriddhi Yojana (SSY)**: A savings scheme for the girl child, offering tax benefits under Section 80C.
4. **National Pension System (NPS)**: A pension scheme that offers tax benefits under Section 80C and an additional deduction of up to Rs 50,000 under Section 80CCD(1B).
5. **Sovereign Gold Bonds (SGB)**: Bonds denominated in grams of gold, offering tax benefits on capital gains.
6. **Senior Citizen Savings Scheme (SCSS)**: A savings scheme for senior citizens, offering tax benefits and a higher interest rate.
7. **Atal Pension Yojana (APY)**: A pension scheme for unorganized sector workers, offering tax benefits.
8. **Pradhan Mantri Jan Dhan Yojana (PMJDY)**: A financial inclusion scheme that provides savings accounts with no minimum balance requirement.
9. **Kisan Vikas Patra (KVP)**: A savings certificate scheme that doubles the invested amount in 113 months, offering tax benefits.
10. **Post Office Time Deposit Account**: A fixed deposit scheme with varying tenures and tax benefits.

Tax Benefits

11. **Section 80C**: Allows for deductions up to Rs 1.5 lakh on investments in specified instruments like PPF, NSC, and ELSS (Equity Linked Savings Schemes).
12. **Section 80CCD(1B)**: Offers an additional deduction of up to Rs 50,000 for contributions to the NPS.
13. **Section 80D**: Provides deductions for health insurance premiums paid for self, spouse, children, and parents.
14. **Section 80G**: Allows deductions for donations made to specified funds and charitable institutions.

15. **Standard Deduction**: Increased to Rs 75,000 from Rs 50,000 under the new tax regime.
16. **New Income Tax Slabs**: The new tax regime introduced in Budget 2024 offers lower tax rates with fewer deductions.
17. These schemes and tax benefits can help middle-class investors save on taxes and build a secure financial future.

References

Chapter 1

1. McKinsey Global Institute. "India's Middle Class: The Next Billion Consumers." McKinsey & Company, 2023. (https://www.mckinsey.com).
2. Economic Survey of India. "Economic Survey 2022-2023." Ministry of Finance, Government of India. (https://www.indiabudget.gov.in).
3. Nielsen India. "The Rise of the Indian Middle Class." Nielsen Report, 2022. (https://www.nielsen.com).
4. Reserve Bank of India (RBI). "India's Economic Development: A Historical Perspective." RBI Bulletin, 2023. (https://www.rbi.org.in).

Chapter 2

1. Kahneman, Daniel, and Amos Tversky. "Prospect Theory: An Analysis of Decision under Risk." Econometrica, vol. 47, no. 2, 1979, pp. 263-292.
2. Banerjee, Abhijit, and Esther Duflo. "The Economic Lives of the Poor." Journal of Economic Perspectives, vol. 21, no. 1, 2007, pp. 141-167.
3. Mohan, Rakesh. "Economic Reforms and the Growth of the Middle Class in India." Economic and Political Weekly, vol. 50, no. 12, 2015, pp. 46-55.
4. Nair, Aparna. "Changing Attitudes Towards Investment: The Case of India." International Journal of Financial Studies, vol. 10, no. 4, 2022, pp. 58-75.

Chapter 3

1. Reserve Bank of India. "Interest Rates on Deposits." RBI, 2023. (https://www.rbi.org.in)
2. World Gold Council. "Gold Investment: An Introduction." WGC, 2023. (https://www.gold.org)

3. Ghosh, Subrata. "Gold as an Investment Asset." Economic and Political Weekly, vol. 56, no. 8, 2021, pp. 45-53.
4. Securities and Exchange Board of India. "Mutual Funds." SEBI, 2023. (https://www.sebi.gov.in)
5. National Stock Exchange of India. "Equity Market Overview." NSE, 2023. (https://www.nseindia.com)
6. Bombay Stock Exchange. "Stock Market Basics." BSE, 2023. (https://www.bseindia.com)
7. Royal Institution of Chartered Surveyors. "Real Estate Investment." RICS, 2023. (https://www.rics.org)
8. International Real Estate Review. "Trends in Real Estate Investment." IRR, vol. 26, no. 1, 2023, pp. 67-82.
9. CoinDesk. "Cryptocurrency Market Overview." CoinDesk, 2023. [https://www.coindesk.com] (https://www.coindesk.com)
10. CryptoCompare. "Understanding Cryptocurrencies." CryptoCompare, 2023. (https://www.cryptocompare.com)

Chapter 4

1. OECD. "Financial Education for Youth." OECD, 2023. [https://www.oecd.org] (https://www.oecd.org)
2. Lusardi, A., & Mitchell, O. S. "The Economic Importance of Financial Literacy: Theory and Evidence." Journal of Economic Literature, vol. 52, no. 1, 2014, pp. 5-44.
3. National Centre for Financial Education. "Financial Literacy Programs." NCFE, 2023. (https://www.ncfe.org.in)
4. SEBI. "Financial Literacy Initiatives." Securities and Exchange Board of India, 2023. (https://www.sebi.gov.in)
5. RBI. "Financial Education and Literacy." Reserve Bank of India, 2023. (https://www.rbi.org.in)
6. Investopedia. "Online Financial Education Resources."

Investopedia, 2023. (https://www.investopedia.com)
7. CFP Board. "Role of Financial Advisors." CFP Board, 2023. (https://www.cfp.net)
8. FPA. "The Value of Financial Planning." Financial Planning Association, 2023. (https://www.onefpa.org)
9. Merrill Lynch. "The Importance of Financial Advisors." Merrill Lynch, 2023. (https://www.ml.com)
10. Bombay Stock Exchange. "Digital Trading Platforms." BSE, 2023. (https://www.bseindia.com)
11. National Stock Exchange of India. "Digital Investment Trends." NSE, 2023. (https://www.nseindia.com)
12. Betterment. "Robo-Advisors Explained." Betterment, 2023. (https://www.betterment.com)
13. Wealthfront. "Automated Investment Management." Wealthfront, 2023. (https://www.wealthfront.com)
14. Finfluencers. "Impact of Financial Influencers on Investing." Finfluencers, 2023. (https://www.finfluencers.com)
15. Forbes. "Financial Influencers and Social Media." Forbes, 2023. (https://www.forbes.com)
16. Harvard Business Review. "Risks of Social Media in Investing." HBR, 2023. (https://www.hbr.org)

Chapter 5

1. Income Tax Department, Government of India. (2021). Tax Benefits on Investments under Section 80C. Available at https://www.incometaxindia.gov.in.
2. Ministry of Finance, Government of India. (2018). Union Budget 2018-19: Introduction of Long-Term Capital Gains Tax. Available at https://www.indiabudget.gov.in..
3. Ministry of Housing and Urban Affairs, Government of India. (2020). Pradhan Mantri Awas Yojana: Guidelines for Credit-Linked Subsidy Scheme. Available at https://pmaymis.gov.in.

4. Reserve Bank of India (RBI). (2019). Report on Agricultural Credit and Subsidies. Available at https://rbi.org.in.
5. Securities and Exchange Board of India (SEBI). (2020). Annual Report on Market Regulations and Investor Protection. Available at https://www.sebi.gov.in.
6. Pension Fund Regulatory and Development Authority (PFRDA). (2021). National Pension System: A Comprehensive Guide. Available at https://www.pfrda.org.in.
7. Reddy, Y. V., & Patnaik, I. (2017). Demonetization: To Deify or Demonize? Economic and Political Weekly, 52(3), 20-23.
8. Ministry of Finance, Government of India. (2017). The Goods and Services Tax: An Overview. Available at https://gst.gov.in.

Chapter 6

1. Ramachandran, S. (2020). Homeownership and Social Status in India: A Cultural Perspective. Journal of South Asian Studies, 18(3), 45-59.
2. National Housing Bank (NHB). (2019). Housing Price Index: Trends in Indian Real Estate Market. Available at https://nhb.org.in.
3. Singh, R. (2021). Volatility in Indian Real Estate Markets: An Investor's Perspective. Indian Economic Review, 36(2), 92-110.
4. Ministry of Housing and Urban Affairs, Government of India. (2020). Real Estate Regulation and Development Act (RERA): An Overview. Available at https://mohua.gov.in.
5. Chakraborty, A. (2018). Liquidity Challenges in Real Estate Investments. Financial Journal of India, 12(1), 74-89.
6. National Institute of Urban Affairs (NIUA). (2021). Urbanization and Housing in India: Addressing the

Affordable Housing Gap. Available at https://niua.org.
7. Desai, M. (2020). Property Ownership and Social Mobility in India. Sociological Review of India, 24(4), 56-72.
8. Banerjee, A. (2019). The Generational Impact of Property Ownership in Indian Families. Indian Journal of Social Research, 30(2), 38-54.

Chapter 7

1. Securities and Exchange Board of India (SEBI). "Investor Education Initiatives." SEBI, 2023. (https://www.sebi.gov.in).
2. Association of Mutual Funds in India (AMFI). "Mutual Funds Sahi Hai Campaign." AMFI, 2023. (https://www.amfiindia.com).
3. Reserve Bank of India (RBI). "Report on Trends and Progress of Banking in India." RBI, 2022. (https://www.rbi.org.in).
4. Madhavan, N. S. "The Evolution of Stock Markets in India: A Historical Perspective." Journal of Financial Studies, vol. 15, no. 2, 2021, pp. 45-67.
5. Agarwal, V., & Naik, N. Y. "The Mutual Fund Industry in India: Growth, Performance, and Challenges." Financial Markets and Institutions Review, vol. 28, no. 3, 2022, pp. 123-146.
6. Behavioral Finance Insights. "Understanding Investor Psychology in Equity Markets." Economic and Political Weekly, vol. 56, no. 4, 2023, pp. 87-95.

Chapter 8

1. Reserve Bank of India (RBI). "Gold and India's Economic and Financial System." RBI Bulletin, 2023. (https://www.rbi.org.in).
2. World Gold Council. "India's Gold Market: Evolution and Innovation." World Gold Council, 2022. (https://www.gold.org).

3. Securities and Exchange Board of India (SEBI). "Investing in Gold: Risks and Rewards." SEBI, 2023. (https://www.sebi.gov.in).
4. Choudhury, S. K. "Cultural Significance of Gold in India." Journal of South Asian Studies, vol. 32, no. 2, 2022, pp. 78-90.
5. Kapur, A. "Gold as an Inflation Hedge: A Historical Analysis." Economic and Political Weekly, vol. 57, no. 3, 2023, pp. 123-134.
6. Gupta, R. "The Role of Gold in Portfolio Diversification." Financial Markets and Institutions Review, vol. 29, no. 4, 2023, pp. 56-70.

Chapter 9

1. Reserve Bank of India (RBI). "Household Financial Savings in India: Trends and Patterns." RBI Bulletin, 2023. (https://www.rbi.org.in).
2. National Pension System (NPS). "Retirement Planning: The Role of NPS." Pension Fund Regulatory and Development Authority (PFRDA), 2023. (https://www.pfrda.org.in).
3. Securities and Exchange Board of India (SEBI). "Financial Literacy and Retirement Planning in India." SEBI, 2022. (https://www.sebi.gov.in).
4. Government of India. "Atal Pension Yojana: A Step Towards Financial Inclusion." Ministry of Finance, 2023. (https://www.finmin.nic.in).
5. Sharma, R. "The Challenges of Retirement Planning in India." Economic and Political Weekly, vol. 57, no. 14, 2022, pp. 45-58.
6. Kapur, A. "Pension Schemes and Their Role in Securing Financial Independence in Old Age." Journal of Financial Planning, vol. 30, no. 2, 2023, pp. 78-91.

Chapter 10

1. Reserve Bank of India (RBI). "Technology and Financial

Inclusion: A Study on Digital Platforms in India." RBI Bulletin, 2023. (https://www.rbi.org.in)
2. Securities and Exchange Board of India (SEBI). "Guidelines for Cybersecurity in Financial Markets." SEBI Circular, 2022. (https://www.sebi.gov.in).
3. National Institute of Securities Markets (NISM). "Digital Literacy and Financial Markets: An Overview." NISM Working Paper, 2023. (https://www.nism.ac.in).
4. Zerodha. "The Impact of Mobile Apps on Retail Investing in India." Zerodha Insights, 2023. (https://www.zerodha.com).
5. World Economic Forum (WEF). "The Future of Financial Services: How Digital Platforms Are Reshaping Investing." WEF Report, 2022. (https://www.weforum.org).

Chapter 11

1. Securities and Exchange Board of India (SEBI). "Gender and Financial Inclusion in India." SEBI Bulletin, 2023. (https://www.sebi.gov.in).
2. National Institute of Securities Markets (NISM). "Financial Literacy and Women Investors in India." NISM Working Paper, 2023. (https://www.nism.ac.in).
3. World Bank. "Women and Financial Inclusion: A Global Perspective." World Bank Report, 2022. (https://www.worldbank.org).
4. Groww. "The Rise of Women Investors in India." Groww Insights, 2023. (https://www.groww.in).
5. Harvard Business Review. "The Financial Gender Gap and How to Close It." Harvard Business Review, 2023. (https://hbr.org).

Chapter 12

1. Global Sustainable Investment Alliance (GSIA). "Global Sustainable Investment Review 2023."(https://www.gsiaalliance.org).

2. Securities and Exchange Board of India (SEBI). "Guidelines for ESG Disclosures and Responsible Investing." SEBI Report, 2023. (https://www.sebi.gov.in).
3. National Action Plan on Climate Change (NAPCC). "India's Climate Action Plan." Government of India, 2023. (https://www.moef.gov.in).
4. McKinsey & Company. "The Impact of Fintech on Investment Strategies in India." McKinsey Insights, 2023. (https://www.mckinsey.com).
5. Reserve Bank of India (RBI). "Digital Transformation in Financial Services." RBI Bulletin, 2023. (https://www.rbi.org.in).

ABOUT THE AUTHOR

Bhavesh Parmar

With over 18 years of extensive experience in the realms of banking, finance, investment, and real estate, Bhavesh Parmar stands as a distinguished authority in the financial world. As the Managing Partner at "GODSPEED INVESTMENT AND FINANCE", Bhavesh Parmar has consistently demonstrated an unwavering commitment to excellence, strategic insight, and innovation.

Beginning his illustrious career in the banking sector, Bhavesh swiftly developed a robust foundation in financial analysis, risk management, and client relationship management. His tenure in banking was marked by a keen ability to navigate complex financial landscapes and deliver customized solutions that met the unique needs of high-net-worth individuals and corporate clients alike.

Transitioning seamlessly into the fields of investment and real estate, Bhavesh brought with him a wealth of knowledge and an exceptional talent for identifying lucrative opportunities. His strategic approach to asset allocation and risk mitigation has led to the construction of diversified portfolios that consistently generate optimal returns for clients.

As the Managing Partner at "GODSPEED INVESTMENT AND FINANCE", Bhavesh oversees all facets of the business, from strategic planning and business development to client relations and operational management. Under his leadership, the firm has flourished, known for its innovative financial solutions, insightful investment advice, and comprehensive real estate services.

Bhavesh Parmar holds an MBA in Finance from ICFAI. Driven by a passion for empowering individuals and businesses to achieve their financial goals, Bhavesh is dedicated to providing education and mentorship to those looking to take control of their financial futures. His extensive experience and deep industry knowledge are reflected in every facet of his work, making him a trusted advisor and respected leader.

For more insights and updates, connect with Bhavesh Parmar on LinkedIn www.linkedin.com/in/bhaveshkparmar.

www.ingramcontent.com/pod-product-compliance
Lightning Source LLC
Chambersburg PA
CBHW071416220526
45469CB00004B/1299